EMMANUEL JOSEPH

Blockchain on the Frontlines, Bridging Military and Health Aid in a Digital Age

Copyright © 2025 by Emmanuel Joseph

All rights reserved. No part of this publication may be reproduced, stored or transmitted in any form or by any means, electronic, mechanical, photocopying, recording, scanning, or otherwise without written permission from the publisher. It is illegal to copy this book, post it to a website, or distribute it by any other means without permission.

First edition

This book was professionally typeset on Reedsy. Find out more at reedsy.com

Contents

1. Chapter 1 — 1
2. Chapter 1: The Digital Revolution in Crisis Zones — 3
3. Chapter 2: The Military's Supply Chain Dilemma — 5
4. Chapter 3: Health Aid in the Age of Distrust — 7
5. Chapter 4: Bridging Two Worlds — 9
6. Chapter 5: The Power of Transparency — 11
7. Chapter 6: Real-Time Data in Crisis Response — 13
8. Chapter 7: The Human Element — 15
9. Chapter 8: Scaling Solutions for Global Impact — 17
10. Chapter 9: The Ethics of Digital Aid — 19
11. Chapter 10: Blockchain and Global Health Crises — 21
12. Chapter 11: The Future of Military Logistics — 23
13. Chapter 12: A Vision for the Future — 25

1

Chapter 1

Introduction: A New Frontier in Crisis Response

In an era defined by rapid technological advancement and unprecedented global challenges, the need for innovative solutions has never been greater. From the battlefields of war-torn regions to the overcrowded hospitals in disaster zones, the world's most vulnerable populations often find themselves caught in systems plagued by inefficiency, corruption, and mistrust. These systemic failures not only hinder the delivery of critical aid but also cost lives. Enter blockchain technology—a revolutionary tool that promises to transform how we approach military and health aid in the digital age. This book, *Blockchain on the Frontlines: Bridging Military and Health Aid in a Digital Age*, explores the potential of blockchain to address these pressing issues, offering a vision of a future where aid is transparent, efficient, and equitable.

Blockchain, at its core, is a decentralized and immutable ledger that records transactions in a secure and transparent manner. While it first gained prominence as the backbone of cryptocurrencies, its applications extend far beyond finance. In the context of military and health aid, blockchain offers a way to track the movement of supplies, verify the authenticity of donations, and ensure that resources reach their intended destinations. Imagine a world where every shipment of medical supplies to a conflict zone is traceable in real time, or where every dollar donated to a humanitarian cause can be accounted for without question. This is the promise of blockchain—a promise that has the potential to save countless lives and restore faith in systems that have too often failed those who need them most.

Yet, the adoption of blockchain in these fields is not without its challenges. In regions where infrastructure is lacking or where trust in technology is low, implementing a digital solution can seem like an insurmountable task. Moreover, the ethical implications of using blockchain—such as concerns about privacy and data security—must be carefully considered. This book does not shy away from these complexities. Instead, it delves into the real-world experiences of those who have pioneered the use of blockchain in military and health aid, highlighting both the successes and the setbacks. Through their stories, we gain a deeper understanding of what it takes to bring innovation to the frontlines.

The intersection of military and health aid is a unique and often overlooked space. While these sectors may seem worlds apart, they share a common goal: to protect and preserve human life. Blockchain has the potential to bridge these two worlds, creating interoperable systems that enhance collaboration and efficiency. For example, during a joint military-humanitarian operation in a disaster zone, blockchain could be used to coordinate the delivery of medical supplies, track the distribution of aid, and ensure that all stakeholders have access to accurate, real-time information. This book explores how such collaborations could be scaled to address some of the world's most pressing crises.

Ultimately, this book is a call to action. It is a reminder that technology, no matter how advanced, is only as powerful as the people who wield it. Blockchain is not a silver bullet, but it is a tool—one that, when used thoughtfully and ethically, can transform the way we respond to crises. By bridging the gap between military and health aid, blockchain offers a glimpse of a future where no life is lost to inefficiency or corruption, and where aid reaches those who need it most. This is the vision that drives *Blockchain on the Frontlines*, and it is a vision worth fighting for.

2

Chapter 1: The Digital Revolution in Crisis Zones

The world was changing faster than ever, and nowhere was this more evident than in the realms of military operations and health aid. In the midst of war zones and disaster areas, the need for efficient, transparent systems had become a matter of life and death. Blockchain technology, once synonymous with cryptocurrencies, began to emerge as a potential game-changer. Its decentralized nature promised to eliminate corruption, streamline processes, and ensure accountability. This chapter introduces the reader to the concept of blockchain and its potential to revolutionize how aid is delivered in the most challenging environments.

The military and health sectors, though vastly different, shared a common problem: inefficiency. Supplies were lost, funds were misallocated, and communication breakdowns often led to catastrophic outcomes. Blockchain offered a solution by creating an immutable ledger that could track every transaction or movement in real time. This chapter explores the early experiments with blockchain in these fields, highlighting both the successes and the skepticism it faced. By the end, the reader begins to understand why this technology could be a lifeline for those on the frontlines.

But implementing blockchain was not without its challenges. In war-torn regions, where infrastructure was often destroyed, the idea of relying on a digital system seemed far-fetched. This chapter delves into the practical hurdles, from lack of internet access to resistance from traditional systems. It also introduces the pioneers who dared to dream of a better way, setting the stage for the stories to come.

The chapter concludes with a reflection on the urgency of the problem. In a world where millions were displaced by conflict and disease, the stakes could not be higher. Blockchain was not just a technological innovation; it was a moral imperative. The question was no longer whether it could be done, but how quickly it could be scaled to meet the need.

3

Chapter 2: The Military's Supply Chain Dilemma

Military operations relied heavily on the timely delivery of supplies, from ammunition to medical kits. Yet, the supply chain was often plagued by inefficiencies, fraud, and delays. This chapter opens with a vivid depiction of a battlefield where soldiers waited for critical supplies that never arrived. The human cost of these failures was immense, and the need for a better system was undeniable.

Blockchain entered the scene as a potential solution. By creating a transparent and tamper-proof record of every transaction, it could ensure that supplies were tracked from factory to frontline. This chapter explores how military leaders began to experiment with blockchain, starting with small-scale pilots. The results were promising: reduced fraud, faster delivery times, and improved accountability.

However, the adoption of blockchain was not without resistance. Many within the military establishment were skeptical of relying on a technology they did not fully understand. This chapter delves into the cultural and institutional barriers that had to be overcome. It also highlights the role of young, tech-savvy officers who championed the cause, bridging the gap between tradition and innovation.

The chapter also examines the ethical implications of using blockchain in military contexts. Could a system designed for transparency be used to protect sensitive information? How could blockchain be adapted to the unique needs of the battlefield? These questions were central to the ongoing debate, and this chapter provides a balanced perspective on the challenges and opportunities.

By the end of the chapter, the reader gains a deeper appreciation for the complexity of the problem and the potential of blockchain to address it. The military's supply chain was just one piece of the puzzle, but it was a critical one. The lessons learned here would pave the way for broader applications in the chapters to come.

4

Chapter 3: Health Aid in the Age of Distrust

In crisis zones, health aid was often the difference between life and death. Yet, the system was riddled with inefficiencies and corruption. This chapter opens with a heartbreaking story of a clinic in a war-torn region that ran out of life-saving medicines due to mismanagement. The human toll of these failures was staggering, and the need for a better system was urgent.

Blockchain offered a way to restore trust in the health aid system. By creating a transparent record of donations and deliveries, it could ensure that aid reached its intended recipients. This chapter explores how humanitarian organizations began to experiment with blockchain, starting with small pilot projects. The results were encouraging: reduced fraud, improved efficiency, and greater accountability.

But implementing blockchain in health aid was not without challenges. Many aid workers were unfamiliar with the technology, and there were concerns about data privacy. This chapter delves into the practical and ethical considerations of using blockchain in health contexts. It also highlights the role of innovators who worked tirelessly to adapt the technology to the unique needs of the field.

The chapter also examines the broader implications of using blockchain in health aid. Could it be used to track the spread of diseases in real time? Could it help coordinate efforts between multiple organizations? These questions were central to the ongoing debate, and this chapter provides a nuanced perspective on the potential and limitations of the technology.

By the end of the chapter, the reader gains a deeper understanding of the challenges facing health aid and the potential of blockchain to address them. The stories of hope and resilience serve as a reminder of why this work matters.

5

Chapter 4: Bridging Two Worlds

The military and health sectors often operated in silos, despite their shared goal of saving lives. This chapter explores how blockchain could serve as a bridge between these two worlds. By creating interoperable systems, it could facilitate collaboration and ensure that resources were used efficiently.

The chapter opens with a dramatic example of a joint military-health operation in a disaster zone. Despite their best efforts, communication breakdowns and logistical challenges hampered their ability to deliver aid. Blockchain emerged as a potential solution, offering a way to coordinate efforts in real time.

This chapter delves into the technical and logistical challenges of creating interoperable systems. It also highlights the role of visionary leaders who saw the potential of blockchain to transform the way these sectors worked together.

The chapter also examines the ethical implications of using blockchain in joint operations. Could a system designed for transparency be used to protect sensitive information? How could blockchain be adapted to the unique needs of both sectors? These questions were central to the ongoing debate, and this chapter provides a balanced perspective on the challenges and opportunities.

By the end of the chapter, the reader gains a deeper appreciation for the potential of blockchain to bridge the gap between military and health aid.

The stories of collaboration and innovation serve as a reminder of what is possible when we work together.

6

Chapter 5: The Power of Transparency

Transparency was a cornerstone of trust, yet it was often elusive in both military and health aid operations. This chapter opens with a stark example of how lack of transparency led to the misallocation of resources during a humanitarian crisis. The consequences were dire, and the need for a better system was clear. Blockchain emerged as a tool to bring transparency to these opaque processes, offering a way to track every transaction and movement in real time.

The chapter explores how blockchain's immutable ledger could be used to create accountability in supply chains. For the military, this meant ensuring that equipment and supplies reached the frontlines without diversion. For health aid organizations, it meant guaranteeing that donations were used as intended. The chapter highlights early successes, such as a pilot program that used blockchain to track medical supplies in a conflict zone, reducing losses and improving delivery times.

However, transparency was not without its challenges. In some cases, revealing too much information could compromise security or privacy. This chapter delves into the delicate balance between transparency and confidentiality, exploring how blockchain could be adapted to meet the unique needs of each sector. It also examines the role of encryption and other technologies in safeguarding sensitive data.

The chapter concludes with a reflection on the broader implications of transparency. Beyond improving efficiency, blockchain had the potential to restore public trust in institutions that had been plagued by corruption and mismanagement. The stories of success served as a reminder of why this work mattered, and the reader is left with a sense of hope for the future.

7

Chapter 6: Real-Time Data in Crisis Response

In a crisis, every second counted. Whether it was a natural disaster or a military conflict, the ability to access and share real-time data could mean the difference between life and death. This chapter opens with a gripping account of a disaster response effort hampered by outdated information systems. The delays were costly, and the need for a better solution was urgent.

Blockchain offered a way to create a decentralized, real-time data-sharing system. This chapter explores how blockchain could be used to track the movement of supplies, monitor the spread of diseases, and coordinate response efforts. It highlights a case study where blockchain was used to track the distribution of vaccines during a disease outbreak, ensuring that doses were delivered to the right places at the right time.

But implementing real-time data systems was not without challenges. In many crisis zones, internet access was limited or nonexistent. This chapter delves into the technical hurdles of using blockchain in low-connectivity environments, exploring solutions such as offline transactions and mesh networks. It also examines the role of partnerships between tech companies and humanitarian organizations in overcoming these barriers.

The chapter also explores the ethical implications of real-time data sharing.

How could privacy be protected in a system designed for transparency? What safeguards were needed to prevent misuse of sensitive information? These questions were central to the ongoing debate, and this chapter provides a balanced perspective on the challenges and opportunities.

By the end of the chapter, the reader gains a deeper understanding of the potential of blockchain to transform crisis response. The stories of innovation and resilience serve as a reminder of what is possible when technology is used for good.

8

Chapter 7: The Human Element

Technology alone could not solve the world's problems; it required the human element to bring it to life. This chapter opens with a poignant story of a health worker in a refugee camp who used a blockchain-based system to track medical supplies. Her dedication and ingenuity were a testament to the power of human resilience, and the chapter explores how blockchain could empower individuals on the frontlines.

The chapter delves into the importance of training and education in the adoption of blockchain technology. Many aid workers and military personnel were unfamiliar with the technology, and its success depended on their ability to use it effectively. This chapter highlights initiatives to provide training and support, from online courses to hands-on workshops. It also examines the role of local communities in adapting blockchain to their unique needs.

But the human element was not just about training; it was also about trust. This chapter explores how blockchain could build trust between stakeholders, from donors to recipients. It highlights a case study where blockchain was used to create a transparent donation system, allowing donors to see exactly how their contributions were being used. The result was a surge in donations and a renewed sense of hope.

The chapter also examines the challenges of maintaining the human element in a digital system. How could blockchain be designed to prioritize human dignity and agency? What safeguards were needed to ensure that technology served people, not the other way around? These questions were central to the ongoing debate, and this chapter provides a nuanced perspective on the ethical considerations.

By the end of the chapter, the reader gains a deeper appreciation for the role of the human element in the adoption of blockchain technology. The stories of courage and compassion serve as a reminder of why this work matters.

9

Chapter 8: Scaling Solutions for Global Impact

The potential of blockchain was immense, but scaling it for global impact was a daunting challenge. This chapter opens with a reflection on the lessons learned from early pilot projects. While these initiatives had shown promise, they were often limited in scope and scale. The question was how to take these successes and apply them on a global level.

The chapter explores the technical and logistical challenges of scaling blockchain solutions. From infrastructure limitations to regulatory hurdles, the barriers were significant. It highlights the role of partnerships between governments, NGOs, and tech companies in overcoming these challenges. It also examines the importance of standardization and interoperability in creating systems that could work across borders and sectors.

But scaling was not just about technology; it was also about culture. This chapter delves into the cultural and institutional barriers to adoption, from resistance to change to lack of awareness. It highlights the role of advocacy and education in building support for blockchain solutions. It also examines the importance of local leadership in driving change from the ground up.

The chapter also explores the ethical implications of scaling blockchain solutions. How could equity be ensured in a system that required access to technology? What safeguards were needed to prevent misuse or exploitation? These questions were central to the ongoing debate, and this chapter provides a balanced perspective on the challenges and opportunities.

By the end of the chapter, the reader gains a deeper understanding of the complexities of scaling blockchain solutions. The stories of collaboration and innovation serve as a reminder of what is possible when we work together.

10

Chapter 9: The Ethics of Digital Aid

As blockchain technology gained traction in military and health aid, ethical questions began to emerge. This chapter opens with a thought-provoking scenario: a blockchain system designed to track aid deliveries inadvertently exposed sensitive information about vulnerable populations. The incident sparked a debate about the ethical implications of using technology in humanitarian contexts.

The chapter delves into the core ethical dilemmas surrounding blockchain. While the technology promised transparency and accountability, it also raised concerns about privacy, consent, and data ownership. How could blockchain be designed to protect the rights of individuals, especially in conflict zones or refugee camps? This chapter explores the importance of incorporating ethical principles into the design and implementation of blockchain systems.

One of the key challenges was balancing transparency with confidentiality. For example, while donors wanted to see how their contributions were being used, recipients had a right to privacy. This chapter examines innovative solutions, such as zero-knowledge proofs, that allowed for verification without revealing sensitive details. It also highlights the role of ethical frameworks and guidelines in shaping the use of blockchain in aid.

The chapter also explores the broader implications of digital aid. Could blockchain exacerbate existing inequalities by excluding those without access to technology? How could the technology be adapted to ensure inclusivity and equity? These questions were central to the ongoing debate, and this chapter provides a nuanced perspective on the ethical considerations.

By the end of the chapter, the reader gains a deeper understanding of the ethical challenges and opportunities of using blockchain in aid. The stories of ethical innovation serve as a reminder of the importance of putting people first in the digital age.

11

Chapter 10: Blockchain and Global Health Crises

The world had witnessed the devastating impact of global health crises, from pandemics to disease outbreaks in conflict zones. This chapter opens with a vivid account of a health worker struggling to coordinate vaccine distribution during a pandemic. The chaos and inefficiency highlighted the urgent need for a better system. Blockchain emerged as a potential solution, offering a way to track vaccines, monitor outbreaks, and coordinate response efforts in real time.

The chapter explores how blockchain could be used to address the unique challenges of global health crises. For example, it could create a tamper-proof record of vaccine shipments, ensuring that doses were not diverted or counterfeited. It could also facilitate data sharing between health organizations, enabling a faster and more coordinated response. This chapter highlights a case study where blockchain was used to track the distribution of vaccines during a disease outbreak, significantly improving efficiency and accountability.

But implementing blockchain in global health was not without challenges. Many health systems were fragmented and underfunded, making it difficult to adopt new technologies. This chapter delves into the practical hurdles, from infrastructure limitations to resistance from traditional systems. It also examines the role of partnerships between governments, NGOs, and tech companies in overcoming these barriers.

The chapter also explores the ethical implications of using blockchain in global health. How could privacy be protected in a system designed for transparency? What safeguards were needed to prevent misuse of sensitive health data? These questions were central to the ongoing debate, and this chapter provides a balanced perspective on the challenges and opportunities.

By the end of the chapter, the reader gains a deeper appreciation for the potential of blockchain to transform global health. The stories of innovation and resilience serve as a reminder of what is possible when technology is used for good.

12

Chapter 11: The Future of Military Logistics

Military logistics had always been a complex and high-stakes endeavor, but the digital age brought new challenges and opportunities. This chapter opens with a dramatic example of a military operation that was delayed due to logistical failures. The consequences were severe, and the need for a better system was clear. Blockchain emerged as a potential solution, offering a way to streamline supply chains, improve communication, and enhance security.

The chapter explores how blockchain could revolutionize military logistics. For example, it could create a transparent and tamper-proof record of supply movements, ensuring that equipment and supplies reached the frontlines without diversion. It could also facilitate real-time communication between units, improving coordination and reducing the risk of errors. This chapter highlights a case study where blockchain was used to track the delivery of medical supplies to a conflict zone, significantly improving efficiency and accountability.

But implementing blockchain in military logistics was not without challenges. Many military systems were highly centralized and resistant to change. This chapter delves into the cultural and institutional barriers to adoption, from skepticism about new technologies to concerns about security. It also examines the role of innovation hubs and pilot programs in driving change within the military.

The chapter also explores the ethical implications of using blockchain in military contexts. How could transparency be balanced with the need for operational security? What safeguards were needed to prevent misuse of sensitive information? These questions were central to the ongoing debate, and this chapter provides a nuanced perspective on the challenges and opportunities.

By the end of the chapter, the reader gains a deeper understanding of the potential of blockchain to transform military logistics. The stories of innovation and collaboration serve as a reminder of what is possible when technology is used for good.

13

Chapter 12: A Vision for the Future

The journey of blockchain in military and health aid had only just begun, but the potential for impact was immense. This chapter opens with a reflection on the lessons learned from the stories and case studies explored in the book. From improving supply chains to enhancing crisis response, blockchain had already shown its potential to save lives and restore trust.

The chapter envisions a future where blockchain is fully integrated into military and health aid systems. In this future, supply chains are transparent and efficient, crisis response is coordinated and timely, and vulnerable populations receive the aid they need without delay. This chapter explores the steps needed to achieve this vision, from investing in infrastructure to fostering collaboration between sectors.

But the future was not without challenges. This chapter delves into the ongoing barriers to adoption, from technical limitations to ethical concerns. It also examines the role of innovation and leadership in driving change, highlighting the importance of bold ideas and courageous action.

The chapter concludes with a call to action. The potential of blockchain to transform military and health aid was too great to ignore. It was up to individuals, organizations, and governments to embrace this technology and use it to create a better world. The stories of hope and resilience served as a reminder of why this work mattered, and the reader is left with a sense of optimism for the future.

Book Description: ***Blockchain on the Frontlines: Bridging Military and Health Aid in a Digital Age***

In a world where crises seem to grow more complex by the day, the systems we rely on to deliver aid are often stretched to their limits. Supplies go missing, funds are mismanaged, and the people who need help the most are left waiting. It's a frustrating and heartbreaking reality, but it's one that doesn't have to be permanent. *Blockchain on the Frontlines: Bridging Military and Health Aid in a Digital Age* is a book about a technology that could change everything. It's about blockchain—a tool that might sound technical and futuristic but, at its heart, is about trust, transparency, and getting help to where it's needed most.

This book takes you on a journey into the heart of some of the world's most challenging environments: war zones, disaster areas, and refugee camps. It's here that blockchain is being tested as a way to solve problems that have plagued aid efforts for decades. Imagine a system where every box of medical supplies sent to a conflict zone can be tracked in real time, ensuring it reaches the doctors and patients who depend on it. Picture a world where every dollar donated to a disaster relief fund is accounted for, so donors know exactly how their money is being used. That's the promise of blockchain, and this book shows how it's already making a difference.

But this isn't just a story about technology—it's a story about people. It's about the soldiers on the frontlines who need reliable supplies to do their jobs, the health workers in overcrowded clinics who struggle to keep up with demand, and the families in crisis zones who depend on aid to survive. It's about the innovators and visionaries who saw the potential of blockchain and worked tirelessly to bring it to life in some of the most difficult places on earth. Their stories are filled with hope, resilience, and the kind of determination that reminds us why this work matters.

Of course, introducing new technology into complex, high-stakes environments isn't easy. This book doesn't shy away from the challenges. It explores the hurdles of implementing blockchain in places where internet access is limited, where trust in technology is low, and where the stakes are life and

CHAPTER 12: A VISION FOR THE FUTURE

death. It also tackles the ethical questions that come with using blockchain: How do we protect people's privacy while making systems more transparent? How do we ensure that technology serves everyone, not just those with access to the latest tools? These are tough questions, but they're essential to getting it right.

Blockchain on the Frontlines is more than just a book—it's a call to action. It's a reminder that technology, no matter how advanced, is only as powerful as the people who wield it. Blockchain isn't a magic solution, but it's a tool that, when used thoughtfully and ethically, can transform the way we respond to crises. By bridging the gap between military and health aid, blockchain offers a glimpse of a future where no life is lost to inefficiency or corruption, and where aid reaches those who need it most. This is the vision that drives this book, and it's a vision worth fighting for.

www.ingramcontent.com/pod-product-compliance
Lightning Source LLC
LaVergne TN
LVHW010444070526
838199LV00066B/6188